L 8/15

WITHDRAWN
26/6/23 SM

D0297142

8

REDCAR & CLEVELAND COLLEGE LIBRARY

362.29309

THE

MYSTIQUE
OF OPIUM

IN HISTORY AND ART

Text: Donald Wigal
Layout: Baseline Co. Ltd
19-25 Nguyen Hue Blvd, District 1, Ho Chi Minh
City, Vietnam

ISBN 1-85995-915-6

© 2004 Confidential Concepts, worldwide, USA
© 2004 Parkstone Press Ltd, New York, USA
© 2004 Cocteau, Artists Rights Society, New
    York, USA / ADAGP, Paris
© 2004 F. Devos (Photographs pp.18, 28, 29,
    30, 31, 32, 33, 36, 37, 38, 40, 42, 43, 44, 45,
    46, 48, 49, 51, 52, 56, 57, 63, 75, 76)

Printed in France

All rights reserved. No part of this publication
may be reproduced or adapted without the
permission of the copyright holder, throughout
the world. Unless otherwise specified, copyright
on the works reproduced lies with the respective
photographers. Despite intensive research, it has
not always been possible to establish copyright
ownership. Where this is the case, we would
appreciate notification.

THE
MYSTIQUE
OF OPIUM

IN HISTORY AND ART

Donald Wigal

ACKNOWLEDGEMENTS AND DEDICATION

Art research by *Jim Cullina* of ArtSleuth, Ontario, Canada; *Anthony Bautista* and *William Kuhns* for providing extensive reference materials; *Fr. James Heft, S.M.* and *John Spellman* for advice; *Joseph Maurer* for generous support; *Mariena Montoya* for office management; *Mel Kuhbander* for sharing his eye for detail; *James Robert Parish* and *George Sullivan* for advice; and especially to *Catherine O'Reilly* for indispensable editorial assistance.

My work here is dedicated to past and present colleagues who are or have been addicted to religion or drugs.

— Donald Wigal, February, 2004

Special thank to Mr and Mrs de Corbez for their photographs.

CONTENTS

I. TURNING ON: INTRODUCTION

THE BEAUTIFUL – AND DANGEROUS

"Drugs were just the beginning."
Advertising tag line, "Traffic: The Miniseries"

Intense interest in the opium clipper, *The Frolic,* started in 1984, with a surprising discovery in the Redwood Forest of California, off the coast of northern California at Mendocina. Pieces of Chinese ceramics which had been shaped into arrowheads by Native Americans were found. The sharpened pieces were discovered among the many boxes of Chinese products from *The Frolic* that were intended to be sold to "the '49ers," those optimistic miners who rushed to California seeking gold in the mid-19th century. [1*]

The clipper had spent its previous six years smuggling North Indian opium from Bombay into China. The Baltimore-built ship was designed to be exceptionally fast. It could do an amazing 14-15 knots, making it capable of escaping the best of Chinese vessels. *The Frolic* was the last of the ships out of Baltimore that embarrassed the slower British ships during the War of 1812. [10]

Driving along the California coast today, thrill seekers might enjoy finding poppies growing wild. What could be more exciting than to find something that could produce the miraculous drug that is praised by scholars and poets, physicians and hedonists throughout history? It could be like the excitement Native Americans probably experienced 150 years ago when they found the treasure from *The Frolic.*

Opium has definitely been shown to relieve pain, reduce hunger and thirst, induce restful sleep and reduce anxiety. However, like other great gifts to mankind, opium can either be of great benefit or be fatal, depending on how, when, and why people use it.

{*} Numbers refer to references listed in the appendix.

J. Le Moyne de Morgues,
Opium Poppy *(Papaver Somniferum)*, c. 1568.
Victoria and Albert Museum, London.

The California dreamers who pick up wild poppies from the side of the road will be brought back to reality after a little research. They will discover that the so-called California poppy [*Escholtzia californica*] is in fact a wildflower in the buttercup family. It produces no capsule and therefore is not actually a member of the poppy family, albeit at frst glance it certainly looks like its capsule-bearing cousin.

Obviously some basic facts and an appreciation about the poppy and opium are needed, even though surely most people have learned some basics already from everyday pop culture. It is almost impossible to watch recent mainstream movies or read pulp fiction without learning that opium is a narcotic drug.

When it was studied more closely, researchers learned that opium is obtained from the juice of the immature fruits of the Oriental poppy. Careful observers will notice that typical opium poppies have four petals of white, violet, pink, or red. They surround a star-shaped stigma from which at least five and up to 16 'rays' fan out. A single pistil [containing from 150 to 200 stamens] is surrounded by five concentric circles. Fertilization produces from 800 to 2,000 seeds. [12]

The true opium producing plant, *Papaver somniferum L.,* is a member of the poppy family *Papaveraceae*. There are over 100 species in that family, several with many varieties. Most are found in temperate Asia and in central and southern Europe, not in the fields of California.

When opium-bearing poppies are studied, many varieties used for the production of poppy seeds and seed oil for baking are not included. Only a few of the many species of poppy contain the alkaloids found in opium. [20]

The clipper Ly-ee-moon.
The London Illustrated News, July 14th 1860, p.37.

Opium Poppy, (three varieties), *Papaver somniferum;*
Field Poppy, *Papaver rhoeas*. 16th century. Watercolor.
Collection of Theodorus Clutius.

Morphine and codeine are two of the most familiar and useful of some twenty natural alkaloids of opium. Several synthetic drugs have been developed from opium, including *meperideine*, best known as Demerol™. It acts more quickly, but its effects are of less duration than morphine. It too is a narcotic and is habit-forming. Paregoric and laudanum also need to be mentioned. [39]

Heroin, *Diacetylmorphine*, was discovered in 1898. It would become the most important drug synthesized from the natural alkaloids. Ironically, heroin was originally thought to be a cure for addiction to other opiates. In the 1860's, the hypodermic syringe was perfected. Physicians mistakenly believed that opium-eating addicts who took morphine by syringe would no longer be addicted to eating opium. Patients with chronic but not life-threatening pain were given morphine and a syringe, with directions on how to inject themselves. But dependence on heroin turned out to be even more devastating than addiction to morphine or opium itself. The great syringe mistake is one example of why science must continually strive to learn. [29, 30]

Paregoric, given to children as well as adults to stop diarrhea, and rubbed onto the gums of teething children, is also an opium tincture, sometimes camphorated. The opium content of camphorated tincture is 25 times less than opium tincture. The way paregoric works is well known. Taking it increases smooth-muscle tone in the gastrointestinal tract. It inhibits mobility and propulsion, thereby diminishing digestive secretions. The liquid form also contains alcohol. Standard nursing handbooks advise that "it can be adjusted precisely to a patient's needs." It is not used as widely today as it once was. [29, 37]

Another form of opium, laudanum, is the modern equivalent of the opium and alcohol mixture that is even mentioned by Homer in *The Odyssey*. As little as two dozen or so drops of laudanum might carry no more than a grain of opium. Laudanum's most notable use is reflected in the work of its most famous users, the most famous of which is Thomas de Quincey.

The mixture was widely prescribed and used in America as well as in Europe, even before Chinese immigrant laborers brought opium with them to the American mines and railroads where they worked. But, as the wave of Chinese people spread east into the United States, so did the establishment of opium dens, followed closely by anti-opium laws. Like the nearly universal presence of prostitution and gambling, and later the consumption of alcohol during Prohibition, the laws concerning opium dens helped create an "open secret" – something nobody denied but also something that nobody admitted to knowing anything about. That is reminiscent of the police in the film "*Casablanca*" who were "shocked" to find gambling in their friend Rick's place.

Pages 10-11: William Alexander, *Chinese Sailor Smoking in His Junk*, 1795.
Watercolor on paper, 22 x 19 cm.
The Makins Collection.

PAPAVER FLORE ALBO

Opium poppy, *Papaver somniferum,* 16th century.
Detail from the previous photo. Watercolor.
Theodorus Clutius Collection.

Red Horned Poppy,
Papaver corniculatum. 16th century. Watercolor.
Collection of Theodorus Clutius.

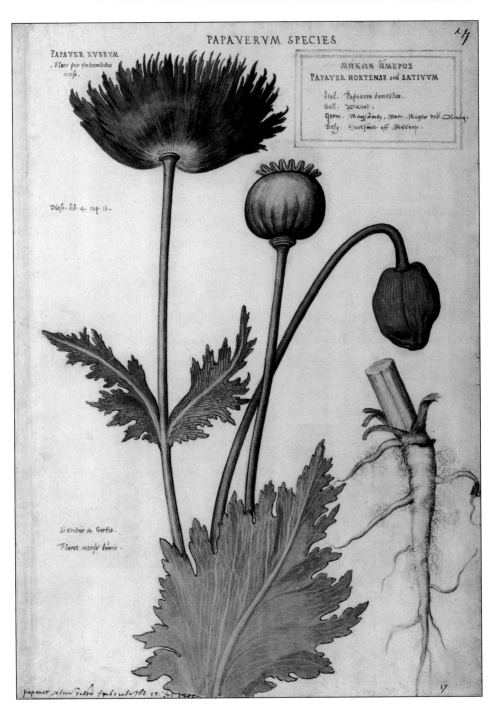

Opium Poppy, *Papaver somniferum*.
16th century. Watercolor.
Collection of Theodorus Clutius.

Francis Croll, *Thomas de Quincey (1785-1859)*, 19th century.
Engraving from a daguerreotype photograph by Howie.
Private collection.

Location for drying the opium.
Engraving from the designs of Lieutenant Colonel Walter S. Sherwill.
The Graphic, 24th of June 1882, p.640.

Pipe, 19th century. 71 cm. bamboo pipe, silver rings, jade tip,
silver plaque decorated with a Fo Dog and Tiger's Eye cabochon.
Yixing terracotta bowl, silver ring.

Pipe, 19th century. 46 cm. Ivory pipe, ivory stopper, silver plaque,
ivory bowl, silver ring. Silver joint ring.
Collection of Pascal Mergez.

DISCOVERING OPIUM: HIPPOCRATES WAS HIP

> "Both as medicine and as holy panacea,
> opium is older than any known god."
> — Nick Tosches

This survey of opium's history begins with a few remotely related facts. The ancient Sumerians referred to the poppy as "the plant of joy." The word poppy is a Latinized form of the Greek, *opion,* as used by Hippocrates four centuries before Christ. Because of its fields of poppies, the Greek town of Kyllene was once known as Poppytown. It was there that a statue in honor of the goddess Aphrodite stood, holding a poppy plant in one of her hands.

Opium might have been introduced into China by Arab importers as early as 400. The practice of 'smoking' opium began about a thousand years later, as early as 1500.

During Europe's great Black Plague, drinking coffee was thought to be a cure for addiction to those who used opium as a painkiller. Some physicians considered both opium and coffee as cures for several ailments. Coffee had invaded Europe from Africa in the early 1600s by way of Venetian traders, then spread to other continents during the decades of expansive colonization. [39, 45]

Near the end of the 17th century, the practice of smoking opium in tobacco pipes was brought to China by the Dutch. By 1750, the use of opium was widespread. The practice expanded to Europe and America during the following century.

Such an innocent looking little plant has played an amazingly influential role in the history of mankind's adventures for "god, glory, and greed." [54]

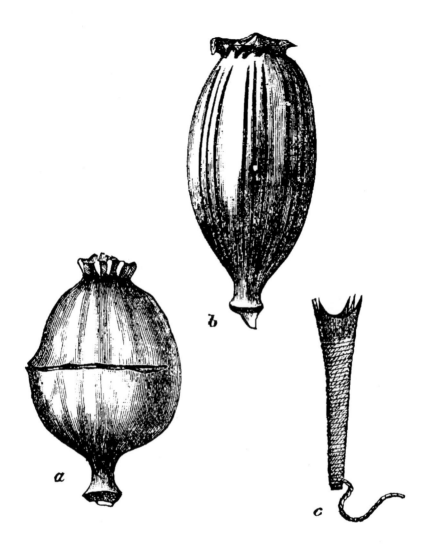

Poppy pods.

Gustave Doré (1832-83), *Opium Smoking – The Lascar's Room*, scene from
'*The Mystery of Edwin Drood*', by Charles Dickens, illustrated in '*London,
a Pilgrimage*', written by William Blanchard Jerrold (1826-94), engraved by A. Doms,
1872. Engraving. Central Saint Martins College of Art and Design, London, UK.

The British Bombardment of Canton.
Excerpt from the *Ridpath's History of the World*,
vol.4, 1899, p.810.

FOLLOW THE MONEY: THE OPIUM WARS

"They fought us with opium. And we are going
to fight them back with their own weapons."
— Chou En-lai

The opening text of the television movie, "Traffic: The Miniseries," neatly summed up centuries of smuggling activity. "For most of recorded history, the wealth of the world came from Asia, reaching the West by sea routes and across remote deserts through desolate mountain pathways. It was guarded by private armies that made their own laws. At first the route carried furs, silks and spices. Later it was to use transporting opium, hashish and heroin by drug smugglers." [45]

Although students in the West usually learn something about such smuggling and the Opium Wars, details of the horrors of such traffic, and especially the wars, are probably minimized. The following is a brief review of the highlights of the wars.

In 1840, England began making a series of bloody mistakes. The Empire was experiencing a serious imbalance of trade as Chinese imports were disproportionately more than England's exports to China.

Even though some respected drug experts in England warned their country against importing opium into England, the unfortunate economy-driven solution was made to pour opium from India into China. England knew the drug was illegal in China. Nonetheless they forced the import of the drug, thus intensifying a demand for their addictive product. England then tried to make a profit by selling the drug to the addicted masses. Shortly after, China ordered all British opium destroyed. Some British merchants were killed and England declared war. [42] Two years later China surrendered and was forced to give the important port of Hong Kong to the British.

Opium, still forbidden by the Chinese government, again poured into China. The major trade link to and from the West and China had always been Hong Kong. During its colonization, the main product of Hong Kong became opium. China was forced by the West not only to allow not only opium to be imported, but missionaries were allowed to enter the country as well. The situation literally prepared the world for Marx's famous 1884 comment that *"religion is ... the opium of the people."* [27]

After the Opium Wars, Western missionaries resumed bringing Christianity to the Orient. Several churches were built in China, and congregations grew rapidly throughout the country. Both the government and the locals have considered Western influence to be mixed blessing ever since. [33]

There was a second opium war in 1860, during which the Chinese capital, Peking, was sacked by British troops. In 1898, Britain signed a 99-year lease under which new territories would also be part of Hong Kong. To take over the area, British troops also defeated armed Chinese peasants.

In 1900, a group of 40,000 militant Chinese called *The Righteousness and Harmony Society*, better known as The Boxers, rose up in China for the purpose of throwing out all Westerners. But England rallied her allies and together they formed 16,000 troops that rather quickly put down what became known as the Boxer Rebellion.

China, rarely a country to move quickly, was to act out some revenge. In 1965, Premier Chou En-lai told President Gamal Abdel Nasser of Egypt: *"Some of them* [the American troops in South Vietnam] *are trying opium, and we* [Chinese] *are helping them. We are planting the best kinds of opium especially for the American soldiers in Vietnam ... Do you remember when the West imposed opium on us* [in the 19th century]? *They fought us with opium. And we are going to fight them back with their own weapon."* [50]

Not only has opium itself played a major role in the history of civilization, but so has opium's natural source, the poppy. In the late 1990s, Afghanistan's Taliban earned worldwide attention with their destruction of statues of Buddha and their harsh laws restricting women's freedom. But they were angry about U.N. sanctions against them, feeling that the world should have congratulated them for eradicating some of the opium-producing poppy crops. [25]

"An opium den in France",
cover illustration for *Le Petit Parisien,* 17th century,
February 1907.

Le Petit Parisien

TOUS LES JOURS
Le Petit Parisien
(six pages)
5 centimes

CHAQUE SEMAINE
LE SUPPLÉMENT LITTÉRAIRE
5 centimes

SUPPLÉMENT LITTÉRAIRE ILLUSTRÉ

DIRECTION: 18, rue d'Enghien (10e). PARIS

ABONNEMENTS

PARIS ET DÉPARTEMENTS :
12 mois, 4 fr. 50. 6 mois, 2 fr. 25

UNION POSTALE :
12 mois, 5 fr. 50. 6 mois, 3 fr.

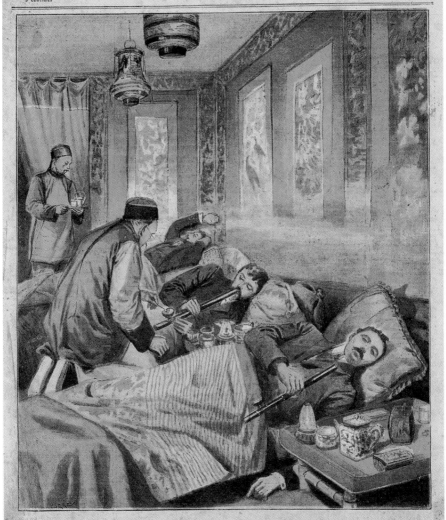

UNE FUMERIE D'OPIUM EN FRANCE

II. TURNING ON: RITUAL AND PRACTICE

INHALING OR SHOOTING UP: POPPY NOSE BEST

"When God put His mouth at the nostrils of Adam,
there was probably opium on His breath."
— Nick Tosches

The young ladies of the opium dens could earn their wages by applying the specialized skills required to master the elaborate preparations needed in producing the pleasant opium vapor as much as they could by being sexually professional. A precise ritual was needed to cause the vapor, requiring an exact amount of heat, as well as very specific instruments and skills.

Using a special lamp and wick was imperative, as were the skills of heating, revolving and shaping the opium, then placing it perfectly into a pipe bowl while holding the pipe at the exact distance from the flame.

When opium burns, it does not actually smoke, but a vapor with qualities distinct from 'smoke' is created. However, referring to the terms 'opium smoke' or 'smokers' is certainly commonly accepted.

There seems to be a real liturgy involved. The ritual acting out, as in superstition, magic and even religion, often seems to be a part of drug-taking behavior. The famous saying of Karl Marx is reversed; we see that opium and other drugs can become the religion of the people.

Léon Busy, *Upper-class woman smoking opium – Tonkin*,
Photography, July-August 1915.

Pages 28-29-30:

Restoration of a tray to smoke Opium, with 19th century objects:

- Bowl, 27 x 6 x 10 cm. Rosewood of Vietnamese origin. Topped by 4 Yixing terracotta bowls. Slide-valve on the back of this object.
- Ashtray, 5 x 3.5 cm Paitung and copper.
- Measure Cask for Opium, 3 x 2.5 cm. Paitung and copper
- Poker in its case, 52 cm long. Brass handle, interior iron handle, interior iron stem, external paitung bowl, set in brass.
- Cure-Bowl, 16.5 cm. wooden handle, iron stem.
- Opium Knife, 14.5 cm. Ivory handle, iron slide.
- Opium Needle, iron, and set with a copper thread.
- Tray, 57.5 x 33 cm. Rosewood.
- Small Tray, 27 x 19.5 cm. Paitung and partitioned enamel.
- Opium Pipe, 60 cm. Bamboo pipe, silver plaque, ivory tip and silver ringed, double stopper one in bamboo and one in silver, representing a lion and a grape; Yixing terracotta bowl.
- Dross spade, 17 cm. Paitung
- Needle Cleaning spade, 8.5 cm, in silvery copper.
- Lamp, 14.5 x 13.5 cm Brass. Topped by a damper and wick (14cm with the chain)
- Opium Box, 4.5 x 4 cm. Copper and Brass.

Outside the tray:
- Water pipe, 24cm.
- Teapot, in tin, interior of double terracotta. Pouring lip and jade handle.
- Saucer, in tin, set in brass.
- Teacup, horn, interior silver finish.

Page 31: Tray, 19th century, 27 x 19.5 cm. Partitioned enamel on copper and paitung.

OPIUM DENS: WHERE EVERYBODY KNOWS YOUR GAME

"I was born to smoke opium in an opium den."
— Nick Tosches

In the popular American television series, *Cheers,* a regular customer was routinely greeted by his first name as he entered the pub, his home away from home. The show's theme song praised such a welcoming place "where everybody knows your name." Appropriately, that bar's most frequent customer's name was "Norm," suggesting it is normal for an individual to want to be accepted by his or her chosen community for who they are.

Opium dens could offer that kind of acceptance. Ironically, the word "den" usually refers to an attractive, domestic place for solitary work or study, whereas some opium dens in contrast were shabby commercial places for individual and social dissipation. Normal people – "Norms" – found their comfort zone.

Sir Arthur Conan Doyle, reflecting his times, refers to the use of opium and heroin in several of his famous Sherlock Holmes adventures, including *The Man with the Twisted Lip, The Sign of the Four* and *A Scandal in Bohemia.* In the first of these, published in 1892, Holmes' loyal colleague, Dr. Watson, visits an opium den in the East End of London to find a friend who is an addict. Booth comments that "the opium den... became an image of transformation from truth into deceit, just as it was for addicted customers who escaped reality there."

The romance of the opium den is vividly described by Nick Tosches: "Visions of a dark, brocade-curtained, velvet-cushioned place of luxurious decadence, filled with the mingled vapor and scents of burning joss sticks and the celestial, forbidden, fabulous stuff itself. Wordless, kowtowing servants. Timelessness. Sanctuary. Lovely loosened limbs draped from the high-slit cheongsams of recumbent exotic concubines of sweet intoxication. Dreams within dreams. Romance." [44]

Opium Pipe. 60 cm. Bamboo tube, silver plaquet,
ivory tip and silver ringed, double stopper one in bamboo
and one in silver, representing a lion and a grape; Yixing terracotta bowl.

Octogonal bowl, 19th century. 7.5 x 7 cm.
Glazed Yixing terracotta. Silver ringed.

HIGHS AND LOWS: A HIP GATHERING

"Opiate – an unlocked door in the prison of identity.
It leads into the jail yard. The Devil's Dictionary
— Ambrose Bierce

The image of the opium den typically shows a user breathing in the vapors of his beloved drug. But why is the user nearly always seen lying on his side?

Pharmaceutical chemist Frank Browne, government analyst in Hong Kong, 1893-1915, describes in detail how opium is prepared and used, but he says nothing more about the opium den than "Opium-smoking is performed by the smoker laying on his side." [4]

The current American writer most "hip" about opium dens is Nick Tosches. He too doesn't really explain why opium smokers lay on their side, but he points out that the word *hip*, as slang for those who are knowledgeable about drugs, dates back to 1904. It "may have derived from the classic, age-old, pelvis-centered, side-laying, opium-smoking position."

The slang may have been code for those who knew the where, how, when, who, if not the why of opium use. Martin Booth, the writer who offers the most comprehensive work on the topic, says the term refers to an experienced drug taker. He adds that "addicts gained sore hips from reclining on their sides on hard, opium den bed-boards. " [5]

A common sense explanation might simply be that inhaling opium vapors can make some smokers too relaxed to stay standing, so it is logical that experienced users would prepare for that state by laying down from the outset. Also, when dining or attending social gatherings in the East, participants are not seated on chairs as they are in the West, but on cushions, maybe even on the floor or ground. The most popular image of "The Last Supper" of Jesus and his apostles is certainly the 1495-97 masterpiece by Leonardo Da Vinci. However, the actual custom of reclining during such feasts, similar to the posture seen in opium dens, is more historically accurate, as shown in the painting of "The Last Supper" by Hieronymus Wierix [1553-1619] at The Fine Art Museum of San Francisco.

A connection between Jesus and opium might be made in the reference in John's gospel [19:29] to the sponge soaked with sour or common wine on a branch of hyssop, given to the crucified Jesus. Some scholars propose that the mixture might have been an opium and wine mixture, used as a painkiller at crucifixions of the time.

Vietnamese bowl, 19th century. 28 x 6.5 cm.
Rosewood, in-laid mother-of-pearl detail.

REDCAR & CLEVELAND COLLEGE LIBRARY

Ashtray, 19th century.

5 x 3.5 cm. Paitung and Copper.

Round opium measure-cask, 19th century.

3 cm high, 2.5 cm in diameter. Paitung and copper.

III. DROPPING OUT:
TABOOS AND FANTASIES

THE EXOTIC APPEAL:
FROM LAUDANUM TO LAURENT

Opium: "God's own medicine."
— Edward Brecher

At certain times and places, especially before medical science better understood the problems of drug-related addiction, drugs enjoyed wide acceptance in general. In fact, some of the substances now considered harmful were once thought to be helpful. Examples range from the innocent to the fatal.

Use of hard drugs was not rare in the upper classes of Victorian England. On the probably harmless side, Queen Victoria's personal physicians prescribed marijuana to Her Majesty for menstrual discomfort. [51]

In France and England, the use of morphine was so common that women would "shoot up" morphine during intermissions at the theater, using beautifully designed syringes that they had customized for just that purpose.

Claims of opium's medicinal power to go beyond the reduction of pain are legendary, but some of those claims have also been proven to be true such as in its effectiveness in helping cure dysentery, asthma, rheumatism, and perhaps even diabetes.

There might be no claims that the scent of opium has therapeutic qualities, but its sweet scent is not unpleasant. Relevant to that quality of the drug, in 1977 the designer Yves Saint-Laurent launched a line of products with the exotic name Opium. The perfume's fragrance is advertised as being "subtle and oriental." It is apparently a blend of rose, carnation, sandalwood, pepper, lily of the valley and clove. While its name and promotion might suggest some of the mystique of the drug after which it is named, the perfume's delightful blend of scent is distinct, though admittedly not an imitation of the sweet and less complex scent of opium.

Opium Box, 19th century.

8 cm high, 7.5 cm in diameter. Partitioned enamel on copper.

THE STORY OF O: CHERCHEZ LA FEMME

> "Not poppy, nor mandragore, Nor all the drowsy syrups of the world,
> Shall ever medicine thee to that sweet sleep
> Which thou ow'dst yesterday."
> — Shakespeare, *Othello*

In the wake of the controversial eugenics debate, it was believed that Orientals were more resistant to opium than Occidentals. Some even mistakenly felt Orientals were more resistant to addiction in general.

In the early 1900s, even some physicians held that certain people are genetically predisposed to addiction. Several agreed with one who opined that the ideal candidate for addiction was "a delicate female, having light blue eyes and flaxen hair, [who] possesses...the maximum susceptibility." [22]

Descriptions of infamous opium dens, past or present, typically include at least one exotic woman. She is usually young, mysterious and subservient to the male opium user. She is usually presumed to be or often is identified as a *fille de joie*. Recently, as if exporting the mystique of the women who worked in the legendary Chinese opium dens, the screen goddess Anna May Wong played an elegant opium-eating Qing Dynasty princess who was transported to Victorian England. [8]

Opium historian Martin Booth notes that such conclusions may have been caused by the fact that morphine was widely used to treat menstrual problems. It was used for "disease of a nervous character" that many people believed women suffered from, and – if some of the trashy romantic fiction about those times is to be believed – women were even *expected* to suffer, especially where being fragile and pampered was considered feminine. Hollywood movies about such women often showed them fainting or swooning for the slightest reason. [5]

Three cure-bowls and a knife.

Needles, 19th century.
18 cm. Iron and enamel traces. The tip set in dross spade.

Lamp, 19th century. 14.5 x 13.5 cm. Brass.
The lamp is topped by a damper, and a wick (14 cm with the chain).

Opium Lamp, 19th century.
11.5 x 6 x 6 cm. Brass and enamelled detail.

The hysterical women of Margaret Mitchell's 1936 novel, *Gone with the Wind*, contrasted with the later more sympathetic descriptions of women of the American southern states.

That was true in Harper Lee's only novel, the 1960 brilliant success, *To Kill a Mockingbird*. The heroine was Caucasian, middle-class and addicted to opium only after it was prescribed for medicinal use.

Morphine was also administered to women as an analgesic during pregnancy and labor. "Furthermore, prostitutes used opiates not only to sustain them in their long and arduous work, but also as a crude form of contraception because continued dosage disrupted ovulation." [44]

Jim Hogshire, an expert on the history of medicines, proposes that one reason women used opium even more than men did in the days of the Industrial-era sweatshops was because women were excluded from public bars, where men could find relief drinking alcohol after their manual labors. He notes that both men and women used opium only when they could not afford gin. Opium was cheaper, healthier and didn't cause fights and hangovers that are so often associated with drinking alcohol. "A night's drinking could easily bankrupt one of these wage slaves, so opium was a staple." [15]

Needle Cleaning spade, 19th century.
9.5 x 3 cm. Large silver.

Smoking Lamp, 19th century,

15 cm x 8 cm in diameter. Brass and receptacle to the copper glass.

Opium Lamp, 19th century. 11 x 7.5 x 7.5 cm.

Detail in partitioned enamel, receptacle to the paitung glass.

Collection of Mr Pascal Merguez.

O, SWEET DEATH: DYING FOR A FIX

"Everything one does in life, even love, occurs in an express train racing toward death.
To smoke opium is to get out of the train while it is still moving. It is to
concern oneself with something other than life or death."
— Jean Cocteau

It is natural to be apprehensive about death, because it is unknown. At most, some have had "near death" experiences. Therefore, maybe only a man of science, when speaking as a scientist, can have the purely scientific objectivity of Bermann Muller [1891-1866]. He dispassionately noted that "Death is an advantage to life ... Its advantage lies chiefly in giving ampler opportunities for the genes of the new generation to have their merits tested out ... by clearing the way for fresh starts." [32]

Spirituality can offer comforting support and maybe can even recommend ways to prepare for death. Religion can also contribute to satisfying the needs of the dying and to help their loved ones. In the prayer, *Ave Maria*, many Christians pray to the Blessed Virgin Mary to "pray for us, now and at the hour of our death." The Catholic liturgy offers *The Anointing of the Sick*, or what was formerly called *Extreme Unction*, one of the sacraments rejected by Martin Luther. Some religious orders use monthly or at least annual prayerful preparations for death, because "we know not the day, nor the hour..." Moreover, the cautious faithful reason that that hour we might not be conscious or otherwise able to pray for ourselves.

Enter the field of bioethics to join moralists in addressing the role of pain relief for the dying. Critical of the restrictive drug laws that make pain relief difficult to get, Nancy Dubler, a lawyer who heads the bioethics division at New York City's Montefiore Medical Center, has stated that 95 percent of pain can be managed. That is the good news. The bad news is that at least 50 percent of patients die in moderate or severe pain. [41]

Elizabeth Ford Pitorak, an expert in end-of-life care at the Hospice Institute at Western Reserve in Cleveland, mentions that "administering morphine or some other opion derivative are the best ways to relieve a [dying] patient's feelings of breathlessness and anxiety." [36]

The fear of death and the preparation for it through pain relief, from mild analgesics to radical anesthesia, seems to show up in personal philosophies. It is seen from the sublime to the ridiculous, from the melancholic soliloquies of Shakespeare's Hamlet,

Pages 48-49: Pipe, 19th century. 71cm.
Bamboo pipe. Yixing terracotta bowl, silver ringed.

De Quincey's "confessions," or the Zen-like poetry of the beat generation, to the rambling, but often insightful, comedy of addict, Lenny Bruce or Richard Pryor. Poet-singer Bob Dylan was "oppressed by fears of dying, since he had to face the fact that he had a following of Messianic proportions." [24] . Throughout much of his lyrics he seems to be constantly aware that he is *"Knockin' On Heaven's Door."*

On the other side of that door there is, according to a popular religious or superstitious notion, a record of one's good and bad deeds. De Quincey came to realize during opium dreams that for him the "The dread book of account is, in fact, the mind itself of each individual." He explained, "This, from some opium experiences of mine, I can believe; I have indeed, seen the same thing asserted twice in modern books, and accompanied by a remark which I was convinced was true: that the dread book of account, which the Scriptures speak of, is, in fact, the mind itself of each individual. Of this at least I feel assured, that there is no such thing as forgetting possible to the mind; a thousand accidents may, and will interpose a veil between our present consciousness and the secret inscriptions of the mind; accidents of the same sort will also rend away this veil; but alike, whether veiled or unveiled, the inscription remains for ever; just as the stars seem to withdraw before the common light of day, whereas, in fact, we all know that it is the light which is drawn over them as a veil - and that they are waiting to be revealed, when the obscuring daylight shall have withdrawn." [9]

In *Man's Fate,* Andrea Mairaux states that "Opium teaches only one thing, which is that aside from physical suffering, there is nothing real." However, just as ecstasy is possible with sex, and some might say it is even more like universal joy, opium seems to offer a glimpse of paradise. After such an experience, the life of the initiate is thereafter wedded to it for richer or poorer, in sickness and in health, till death.

Standup comic sensation Richard Pryor accidentally set himself on fire while "freebasing," that is, preparing a highly volatile cocaine mixture. However, he survived and later recalled the near-fatal experience in a humorous autobiographical routine titled, *"Jo Jo Dancer, Your Life is Calling"* [1896]. He creatively addressed the need to cope with death by using warm wit rather than cold analysis.

Influential comedian Lenny Bruce took a fatal overdose at age 40. "Contrary to mythology, Lenny did not die of an overdose of heroin. He died of an overdose of drugs alright, but it was morphine, and somehow morphine is just not fashionable for myths, the lab report to the contrary notwithstanding." [11]

Of his excessive use of drugs, Bruce once said, "I'll die young, but it's like kissing God."

Opium scale, 19th century. 34 x 9 cm.

Rosewood case, brass studs. Ivory beam. Brass feet and tray.

The scale is used to weigh gold, silver, medicinal herbs, powders and opium.

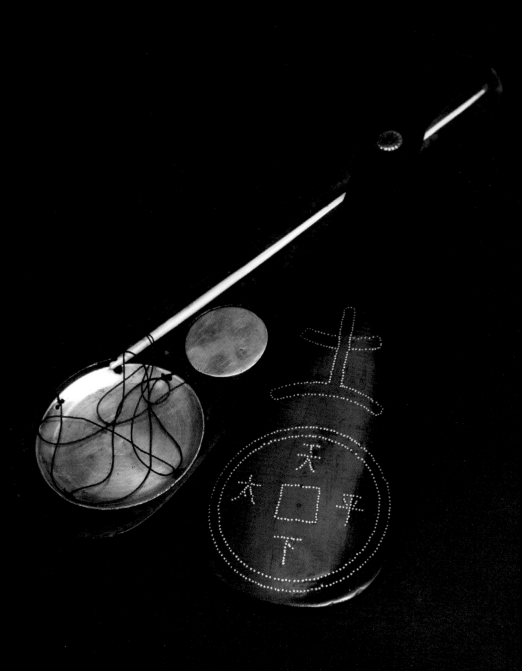

Opium box, 19th century. 49 x 40 x 24 cm. Lacquered wood encrusted
with different coloured mother-of-pearl. This piece of furniture includes three drawers,
four places to support the pipes, and an enclosed place by a door.
This piece of furniture serves to arrange all the necessary tools for smoking opium.

IV. GETTING REAL: OPENING OUT ON REALITY

THE POPPY TRAIL: REPEATING HISTORY

"The opium-eater loses none of his moral sensibilities,
or aspirations...but his intellectual apprehension of what is possible
infinitely outruns his power, not of execution only, but even of power to attempt."
— Thomas De Quincey, *The Pain of Opium*

William Willcox, a notable chemical pathologist in England in the second decade of the 1900s, wrote that there were two classes of drug addicts. The first group included those of the general population who became dependent on prescriptions for medical purposes. Typically those unfortunate addicts took drugs to seek relief from pain or sleeplessness.

But addicts in the other group were hedonists who sought new excitement and pleasure through drugs. Morphine and heroin, as well as cocaine, were taken orally, by injection or inhaled as snuff, and were the drugs commonly used. Wilcox called those in the second category the "vicious groups," but he acknowledged there were other factors that might have contributed to violence.

Some in the first group might have had morphine or heroin prescribed to control pain following a surgical operation. Willcox noted that heroine and morphine "often act as a charm," apparently meaning they seem to have magical qualities.

Therefore, it is understandable that a user can or might get "hooked" rather quickly. Willcox estimated that the daily use of an addictive drug such as morphine or heroin for about four weeks "in most cases" could cause an addiction to develop.

Apparently he was describing addicts of both categories when he wrote that "a family history of insanity, neurosis or of alcoholism is usual amongst drug addicts, and they themselves previous to their addiction often present signs of nervous instability." He also felt that alcohol addiction was frequently combined with that of morphine, heroin or cocaine.

An opium smoker and his material

– two opium and one water pipe, c. 1910.

Rich Chinese men smoking opium in a private room.
Taken from *The living Races of Mankind,* c. 1900, p.211.

Travel pillow chest, 19th century. 51 x 14 x 14.5 cm.

Lacquered leather, gilt traces on the design. Brass hinges.

Even a century ago experts knew that controlling the production of opium and the alkaloids obtained from them would attack the very heart of the "the opium problem." However, they acknowledged that illegal trafficking of opium, morphine, and heroin "undoubtedly occurs to some extent." Willcox believed the new [1920] Dangerous Drugs Acts would bring matters under control. He later even stated that "the number of those actually engaged in it [illegal trafficking] is consequently very small." [56]

In the United States during the 1920s, about 95% of all narcotic addicts used opium in the form of heroin or morphine. The latter group outnumbered heroin users twelve to one. A representative of the U.S. Department of Health, who specialized in the problems of drug addiction, reported that smoking opium had been fairly common, but that it was confined to "a few Chinese in large cities."

That expert also claimed that most "normal subjects" and even many of the "less stable of the abnormal group" who became addicted through self-medication with opium, had been "cured permanently." The rest of the addicts were categorized as an unstable group that constantly relapsed, it was believed, "because of the instability that was the cause of their original addiction." He concluded that many of the unfortunate unstable ones have been *"cured"* ten to twenty times. [35]

There are two highlights in the history of opium during the 1940s. The first occurred in 1945, when American General Douglas McArthur, in charge of occupied Japan, forbade the farmers of that country to cultivate opium and ordered the halting of all narcotic production. The second was in 1949 when the U.N. Narcotics Commission established a committee in Ankara (formerly Angora), Turkey, to control and supervise the trading of opium throughout the world. [23]

Long before the new millennium, Vietnam was clearly identified by anti-drug agencies for playing an increasingly important role in heroin trafficking throughout the 'Golden Triangle,' an imaginary area encompassing parts of southwestern China and northern Thailand.

In Vietnam, possession or smuggling of 100 grams or more of heroin, or five kilograms or more of opium, has been punishable by death since 1997. Death sentences are frequently handed down to heroin and opium traffickers; in 1999, sixty people were sentenced to death for smuggling illegal substances into that country. According to Vietnamese newspapers, about 18,000 people were arrested for their involvement in drug smuggling and drug abuse in the first nine months of 1999 alone. [48]

Inside a grocer's store in San Francisco, no date. Apart from the usual medicaments, herbs and everyday use products, this shop possibly also sold opium.

A new Vice. Le Petit Journal, 5th of July 1903.

THE PEN IN THE DEN: THE BEAT GOES ON

"What part the drug had in the creation of shapes and forms
is evident in the now famous works of
De Quincey, Poe, and Coleridge."
— L. D. Kapoor

In his "ottobiography," as he liked to call it, Otto Preminger tells of how he, actor Gary Cooper and producer-writer Milton Sperling, each asked their physicians for a prescription for Demerol™. However, the doctors knew that the requests were actually being made for screenwriter Ben Hecht. In order to meet the team's pressing deadline, Hecht felt he needed the drug, which he become hooked on after surgery the year before. [40]

To get their work done, or perhaps using writing as their excuse, many famous writers have used alcohol. Some of these called on the help of opium instead, or as well. The following is a list of a few of the many intellectuals, writers, poets, artists, and other creative people who were either users or were otherwise intensely interested in opium or its derivatives. These include writers of the "beat generation" (each indicated with an asterisk).

Apollinaire, Guillaume
Auric, Georges
Baudelaire, Charles
Beardsley, Aubrey
Browning, Elizabeth Barrett
Bukowski, Charles*
Burroughs, William*
Carso, Gregory*
Cassady, Neal*
Cocteau, Jean
Coleridge, Samuel Taylor
Collins, Wilkie
Crabbe, Fr. George
Crowley, Alistare

De Quincey, Thomas
Detzer, Eric*
Dickens, Charles
DiPrima, Diane*
Doyle, Arthur Conan
Dreser, Heinrish
Dylan, Bob*
Ferlinghetti, Lawrence*
Galen
Ginsberg, Allen*
Greene, Graham
Hippocrates
Huxley, Aldous
Jones, Leroi*

Keates, John	Poulenc, Francis
Kerouac, Jack*	Radiguet, Raymond
Kesey, Ken*	Rossetti, Dante Gabriel
Kosterlitz, Hans	Sertürner, Wilhelm
Laloy, Louis	Snyder, Gary*
Linnaeus	Snyder, Solomon
Malraux, André	Sydenhaim, Thomas
Marcus Aurelius	Thompson, Francis
McClure, Michael*	Vlice, Charles
Paracelsus	Ward, Arthur
Pert, Candace	Wilberforce, William
Picasso, Pablo	Wilde, Oscar
Poe, Edgar Allen	

Users of cocaine and other hard drugs, even if just limited to popular musicians, would require a much longer list, of course. Also not addressed here are the LSD-users of the 1960s, many of whom were influenced by Timothy Leary, even before his influential 1968 work, *The Politics of Ecstasy.*

Martin Booth is especially helpful when he shows how opium is presented in the works of certain writers. [5]

The most famous writer who confessed to drug abuse is undoubtedly De Quincey. In 1802, at the age of 17, De Quincey ran away from the security of a stable home. In London, he befriended a prostitute with whom he lived while studying at Worcester College, Oxford.

Quincey took opium for the first time in order to relieve the pain of facial neuralgia. By age 28, he had become a regular and confirmed "opium-eater." He took his "celestial drug" in the form of laudanum, and he always kept a decanter of it nearby and steadily increased the dose. He remained an addict for the rest of his life, dying at age 74 in 1859.

De Quincey's "confessions" were published in 1821, when he was 36. It was, as Martin Booth said, "the first time that opium addiction ... was laid bare in a book in which the author stated opium, rather than himself, was the true hero of the piece." [5]

De Quincey also reflected on the point of how guilty he felt because he neglected responsibilities while under the influence of opium. He is the most famous of opium addicted writers and is eloquent in describing the ecstasy of taking the drug.

Head Rest (or pillow), 19th century.
29.5 x 13 x 13.5 cm. White porcelain decorated in blue.

Head Rest (or pillow), 19th century. 31 x 12 x 11.5 cm.
Red and black lacquered leather, carrying a design gilded in points.

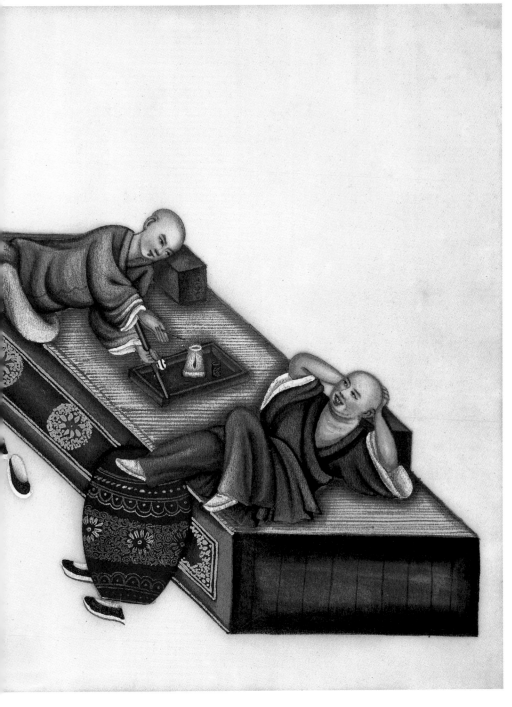

Smokers in an opium den,
from *'The Evils of Opium smoking'*
(bound in an album). Color on paper. British Library, London.

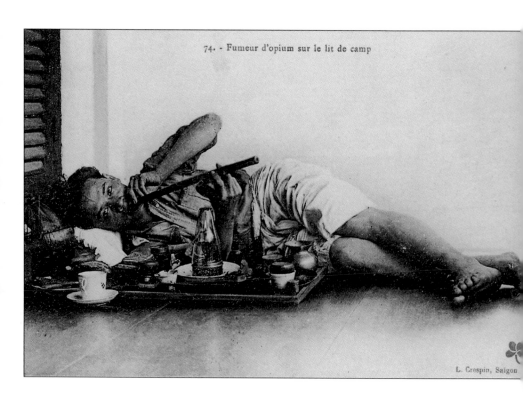

74. - Fumeur d'opium sur le lit de camp

L. Crespin, Saigon

L. Crespin, *Opium smoker reclining*.
Saigon, c.1926. Postcard.

75. - Préparation d'une Pipe d'opium

L. Crespin, *Preparing an opium pipe*,
c.1926. Saigon. Postcard.

Leonardo da Vinci, *The Last Supper*,
c. 1495-97. Oil and tempera on wall, Milan.

Since the 19th century, De Quincey's influential shadow has fallen over subsequent writers. A survey of a few highlights about famous writers who used or wrote about opium continues with Dickens. In his unfinished last novel, *The Mystery of Edwin Drood* [1870], the main character is an opium addict.

Booth mentions, "For Dickens, opium was a symbol of degeneracy, of a surrender of basic human values, a corruption of decency." Dickens himself used laudanum as a cough mixture to help him relax during his speaking tours.

Wilde was also a user of laudanum. The title character of his novel, *The Picture of Dorian Gray* [1891], visits an opium den in hopes of escaping his feelings of guilt. Booth notes, "The opium, from which there was also no escape, is [in this Wilde work] an image of entrapment: no amount of opium can alter the truth."

The range of "confessions" includes Doyle's comparatively subtle references to opium in his Sherlock Holmes adventures. They probably reflect the writer's own addiction.

Arguably the best work of Greene was *The Quiet American*. It was prophetic in describing the failure of U.S. foreign policy in Indochina. The first filmed version of the novel, directed by Joseph Mankiewicz. In the Philippines it was called *"The Spy."*

In Germany it was called *"Der Stille Amerikaner."* A 2002 version, directed by Phillip Noyce, was much less successful, albeit the topic was still timely. Greene first enjoyed opium in 1951, but he was never addicted.

However, he did have a public love-hate relationship with his Catholicism, and might have brought that religion's fascination for ritual and ambience to his worship of *fumeries* [opium dens]. The theme appears most obviously in his 1955 novel, *The Quiet American,* as well as in his 1980 autobiography, *Ways of Escape*.

But even more dramatic evidence of the influence of opium in writing is seen with Coleridge. While still somewhat in an opium dream, he wrote his most famous poem, "Kubla Khan." Several generations later the Beatnik generation would revive this work and call it their own.

Burroughs is now seen to be a prophet not only for his own time but for our time as well, such as in his *"The Last Words of Hasan Sabbah,"* which condemns terrorism, e.g. government intelligence agencies and big business. [31] Burroughs, a seminal voice for the beat generation, coined the phrase "shooting gallery," which he felt described his living room where his fellow addicts met. [5]

Ayer's Cherry Pectoral. Publicity picture.

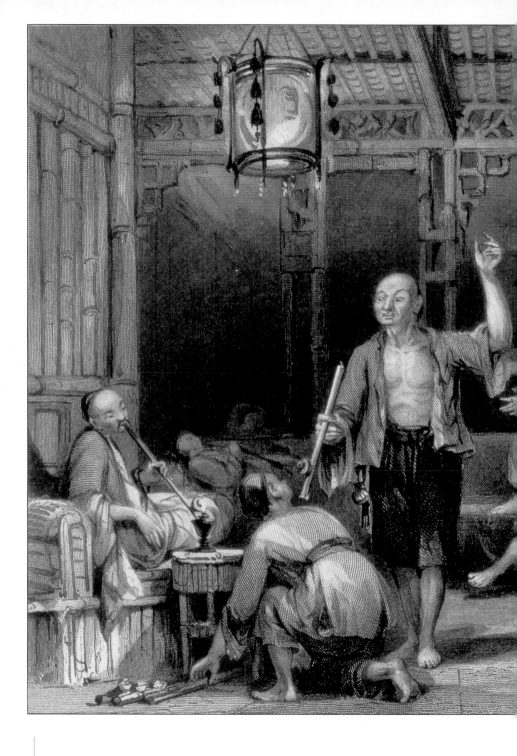

Thomas Allom, *Chinese Opium Smokers*, from *'China in a Series of View'*,
by George Newenham Wright (c. 1790-1877), 1843. Engraving. 1843. Private Collection.

Some biographers claim Burroughs coined the word "beat" itself, but others point to Kerouac as the more likely inventor of the word that describes the movement. Either way it apparently refers to both "beat down" (rejecting conventional consumerism, for example) or to "beatific" (vaguely referring to a non-institutional spirituality possible to achieve through drugs) by the works of Burroughs and the poets Ginsberg, Ferlinghetti and Corso. To some degree, each expressed to some degree an involvement with drugs, a form of Zen Buddhism, contemporary jazz, and "a heightened respect for the individual over the masses." [17]

American writers known as the "beat generation" became prominent, first in New York's Greenwich Village and then in San Francisco. By that time Ginsberg's very popular poem "Howl" [1956] began to be the movement's anthem. He became the Walt Whitman of the beat generation.

Influenced by Burroughs, Kerouac was the influential theorist of the beat generation, particularly as seen in his seminal novel, On the Road [1957]. It was a "major document of beat-generation thinking and writing." [Kerouac typed it onto 20-foot long rolls of poster paper that he taped together forming one continuous manuscript.] Kerouac, whom Booth calls "the archetypal addict writer," was a self-proclaimed mystic or secular contemplative. With a unique and witty voice, he reported on the social disillusionment assuaged by drugs and alcohol. [3]

The poet Bob Dylan was very different kind of spokesman for his generation, but like Kerouac he too knew it was a generation that was disillusioned and felt alienated. [24] Some of his album covers became icons of the age. His interest in drugs was evident in his lyrics, as in "Mr. Tambourine Man."

The most frequently recommended anthology of the beat generation is The Portable Beat Reader [1992], edited by the Kerouac biographer, Ann Charters. But there is no substitute for reading the unabridged works also, especially On The Road.

Sam Kashner is one of the writers who was influenced by the beat founders. Many of the anecdotes included in his work: "When I was Cool" [2004], capture the twilight years of the founders as he knew them in the late 1970s. [20, 21]

He was a student at the Jack Kerouac School of Disembodied Poetics in Boulder, Colorado, where he sat at the feet of Burroughs, Ginsberg, and Corso. Kashner recalls Corso had commented to him over twenty years before, "We're just old men, soon to poof into the air." [28]

But, the beat goes on.

Travelling Pipe, 19th century. 56.5 cm
(in two parts). Pipe in lacquered bamboo, ivory tips,
brass and paitung rings, brass rings joined, paitung tray, Yixing terracotta bowl.

Pipe, 19th century. 36.5 cm.
tortoise shell pipe, ivory tip with silver ring. Hand shaped bowl
made of ivory and silver. Yixing terracotta bowl, white brass metal ring.

POPPY AND POPCORN: FINDING THE O IN MOVIE

"Dare you enter the nightmare zone of the incredible."
Promotion tag line from the movie
"Confessions of an English Opium-Eater"

There have been at least 35 feature movies released between 1890 and 2004 that are specifically about opium, including at least 18 documentaries.

The ones named here are specifically about opium, selected from hundreds of films about addiction that have been made throughout the world. [51]

Even among the very earliest silent motion pictures there was an interest in opium. It was considered an exotic subject. It was perfect for the new medium of 'moving pictures.' A short documentary entitled "Chinese Opium Den," was made in 1894.

Four years later, a two-part documentary entitled "A Chinese Opium Joint" was released. The title referred to a location, not a marijuana cigarette as "joint" later came to be called. There were at least two follow-up documentaries in the next five years.

The French film, "Le Rêve d'un fumeur d'opium" [1908], was known in the U.S. that same year as "Dream of an Opium Fiend." Later presentations that anticipated the more sinister side of opium traffic were dramas about opium smuggling, which were made at least once a year over the next decade. In 1914 the documentary, "The Opium Cigarettes," was released, as was a film informally known to English speaking audiences as "Opium Dreams." The next year the documentaries "Satan Opium" and "Opium" [1919], in the style of German expressionism, would be the final feature films on the topic for over 20 years.

Pipe, 19th century. 36.5 cm.
tortoise shell pipe, ivory tip with silver ring. Hand shaped bowl made of ivory and silver. Yixing terracotta bowl, white brass metal ring.

The 30s film "The Cocaine Fiends" was not a documentary, but was given some attention because movie-goers then were mostly interested in seeking entertainment that would help them, if only for a brief time, avoid the painful realities of the crash of Wall Street and The Great Depression.

It was a time when several classic "escape" movies were successful, including the "Wizard of Oz." In it, the main character, Dorothy, steps into a colorful world where she takes an adventurous and at times nearly psychedelic journey through a poppy field with her friends along the Yellow Brick Road.

With World War II very much on the minds of all movie audiences during the 1940s, the first film about the Opium Wars was released, followed by another in 1943. Similarly, a Chinese documentary film was released in 1959, and was known to American audiences as "The Opium Wars." As expected, the film presents a much-needed Chinese point of view concerning the cause of the Opium Wars.

With Vietnam and real wars dominating the world in the '60s, documentaries about past wars brought realities home, and yet another documentary about the Opium Wars was released in 1964. A 1997 documentary was known in the U.S. as "The Opium War."

The film's story begins in 1839 when British merchants are about to be executed by the Chinese for importing illegal opium into China. A year after the U.S. film, "To the Ends of the Earth" [1948] was released, it was re-titled "Opium" for Austrian and West German audiences. Other films with that same title were released in 1919 [mentioned above] as well as a Russian film with the same name in 1991.

An Austrian film, "Luftfracht Opium" [1958], was a German version of "Tip on a Dead Jockey" [1957], also known as "Time for Action." The German film, "Vier Pfeifen Opium," was also distributed that year.

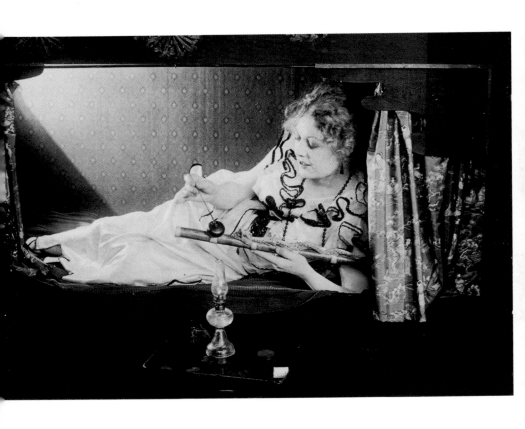

Scene from the film *The Dividend*, 1916.

Edgar Allan Poe, 1884.

Engraving on copper by Richard Henry Stoddard.

Charles Baudelaire.
Extract from *The Feather*, 1st June 1903.

The Albert Zugsmith documentary, inspired by the popular 1821 autobiographical book of Thomas de Quincey, "Confessions of an Opium Eater" [1962], was known in England as "Evils of Chinatown," and was reissued in the U.S. under the unfortunate title "Souls for Sale."

The opium documentary with the most alternative titles and translations is the 1966 film "Poppies Are Also Flowers." It was an adaptation of Ian Fleming's story about U.N. plots to inject radioactive material into opium in hopes that the plant would then lead them to an illegal heroin distributor.

Its alternative title in England was "Danger Grows Wild," and in Austria was "Mohn ist auch eine Blume." Even within the U.S. it had alternative titles, including "The Opium Connection" and "The Poppy Is Also a Flower." A 1972 film known in West Germany as "The Opium Connection" was called "Action héroïne" [1978] in France. In the video edition it is called "La Filière." The dubbed Canadian version of the film is titled, "The Sicilian Connection," [1977] also known as "Opium Connection."

And during the '60s the film was known as "Deadly China Doll" or "The Opium Trail." A 1969 South Korean documentary is popularly known as "Opium Flower."

Few noteworthy feature films about opium were made during the final quarter of the 20th century. One exception is "L'Opium et le bâton," a 1971 film directed by Ahmed Rachedi in Algeria. Very few films deal with the topic in the 1980s. One is a Cantonese movie from 1984 known as "Lightning Fists of Shaolin," or "Opium and the Kung Fu Master."

The Man Who Came Back, (USA, 1930).
With Janet Gaynot, Charles Farrell, Kenneth MacKenna
and William Holden, adapted from Jules Eckert Goodman's play.

REDCAR & CLEVELAND COLLEGE LIBRARY

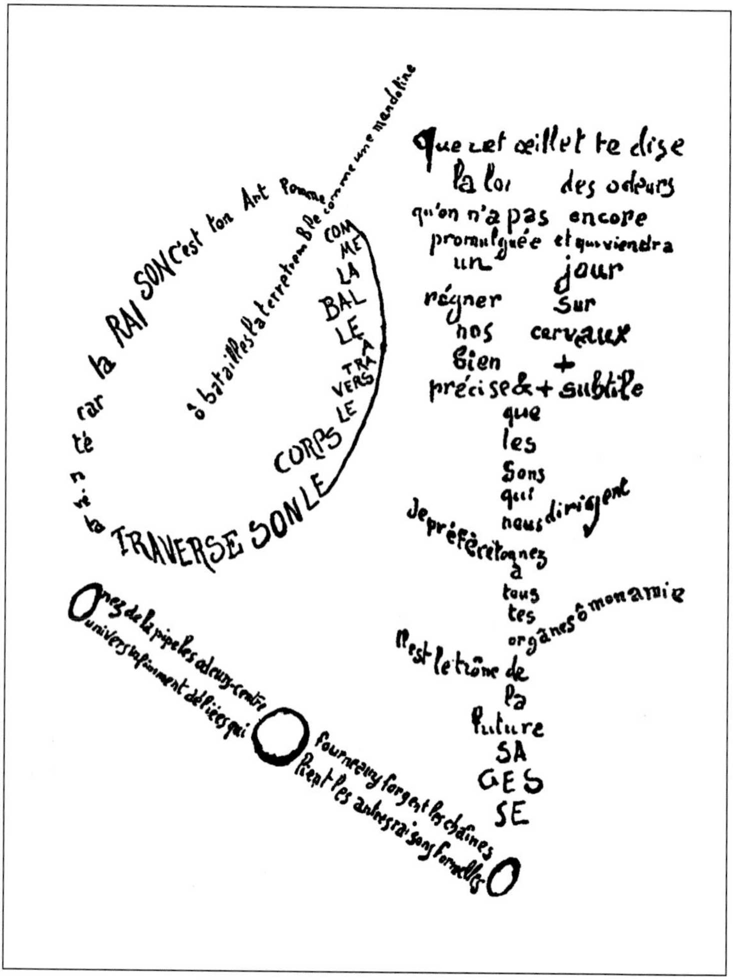

Que cet œillet te dise
la loi des odeurs
qu'on n'a pas encore
promulguée et qui viendra
un jour
régner sur
nos cerveaux
bien
+
précise & + subtile
que
les
sons
qui
nous dirigent
Je préfère ton nez
à
tous
tes
organes ô mon amie
Il est le trône de
la
future
SA
GES
SE

la RAISON C'est ton Art Pomme comme une mandoline

ô batailles la perception De la comme une mandoline

car té n'i te

COM
ME
LA
BAL
LE
A
TRA
VERS
LE

CORPS

TRAVERSE SON LE

rez de la pipe les aleurs centre
univers infiniment delicspi
Pour que vy forgent les chaînes
Rent les autres raisong formelles

As of this writing, the most recent feature film addressing opium is a 2000 Swedish documentary. However, movies about opium that have been made for television include the documentaries "Opium Eaters," [1990] and "L'Opium des Talibans, [2000].

The HBO series, "The Wire," went through an evolution similar to that experienced by the genre itself, shifting its focus from drugs in the first season to trafficking of young prostitutes in the second season.

The theater also often tries to deal with opiates, albeit often with less intimacy than does film. The latter can zoom in on the horrors of an overdose as well as provide an overview of its global impact.

A brilliant exception to this is Eugene O'Neill's four-hour masterpiece, "Long Day's Journey into Night," which critic Clive Barnes once said "just might be the worst great play ever written." Through chilling dialogue, it presents the story a morphine matriarch and her impact on her family. It dramatizes both the physical and psychological ravages of addiction.

The beginning and the next section of this book discuss or analyze the two popular television miniseries and the movie series that deal with the influence of illegal drug traffic, slaves, and weapons on the global economy, as well as the impact on individual lives.

"Drugs were just the beginning," was a timely tag line used by the recent miniseries. It suggests that illegal drugs have contributed greatly to how we each think, act and feel about ourselves and our world.

Guillaume Apollinaire,
"The Mandolin, the Carnation and the Bamboo",
Calligramme, Gallimard, 1925.

BERKLEY BOOKS

G-120

35¢

THE SHOCKING ECSTASY OF THE FORBIDDEN

BLACK OPIUM

Claude
Farrère

COMPLETE AND UNABRIDGED

TRAFFIC JAM: DRUGS WERE JUST THE BEGINNING

"Drugs have been replaced by other things."
— Stephen Hopkins

As previously mentioned, the original routes from East to West were set up in order to trade furs, spices and silk. The routes were later used to transport opium, hashish and morphine. And now in this age of terrorism, the routes are used to transport dangerous weapons from the heart of Asia to nearly every part the Western World.

As of this writing, Taliban loyalists and terrorists threaten stability of Afghanistan's shaky government. Resurgent drug trade ultimately provides funds to terrorists, feeds political unrest, and promotes violence. Paul Barker of CARE reports that over 75% of the world's illegal drug production comes from Afghanistan.

At this time, opium production in Afghanistan is at record high levels, certainly many times more than the needs of legitimate medical industries. NATO reports that there is a "palpable risk that Afghanistan will once again turn into a failed state" due in large part to the influence of illegal drug production. [33]

"Drugs have been replaced by other things," according to director and producer Stephen Hopkins. He states, "drugs have now become the tender to pay for smuggling. The same routes have been used for thousands of years, for slave trading, illegal smuggling of all types.

Cover of the 1958 translation of *Fumée d'opium*.

Obviously, drugs became huge in this last century. Now smuggling immigrants and refugees is a multi-million dollar business." [38]

This short overview of opium's use in the 19th century shows the concern of the civilized world regarding illegal drugs and how territorial conflicts led to *regional* wars. The survey then shows how the focus morphed in the 20th century into concern about this same conflict expanding to *nations*. Now the world must face the challenge of dealing with drugs on a *global* scale to fight terrorism in the 21st century.

The awesome medicinal benefits of drugs derived from opium, and the beautiful artifacts seen on these pages associated with the use of opium, must not hide a brutal reality. Some terrorism is typically funded by illegal trafficking of drugs, of biological and other weapons, of slaves for prostitution, and of illegal aliens. Again, drugs were just the beginning.

What Hopkins said of the television miniseries "Traffic" could be said also of this book: "Maybe it just opens up the boundaries of looking at things. There are no real answers to a lot of these [illegal traffic] problems, so we don't pretend to give them." [38]

The purpose of this informal survey is to encourage thoughtful discussion and appropriate social action that flows from an appreciation for the mystique and important role that opium plays in human history and its art. [52]

Like religion, opium and its derivatives can also be beneficial, beautiful, spiritual, and even channels of ecstasy. Or, again like religion, they can be depressing, destructive, seriously harmful, or even fatal to individuals and to cultures, depending on how they are managed by their worshipping faithful.

In a free society, individual priorities about these very personal matters will vary, but the common good of society must be a factor. Many people can live their lives without either religion or drugs, but lives can be enhanced with their appropriate use.

Opium Den, 614 Jackson Street.

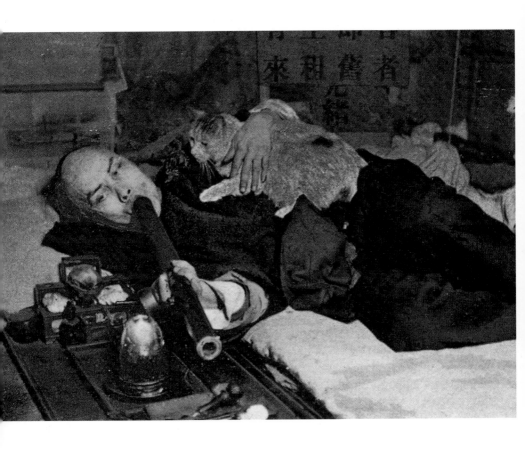

Jean Cocteau, sketch No. 31 for:
Opium : journal d'une désintoxication, 1930.

INDEX

REFERENCES

This list include some of many resources consulted,

but not all are cited in the text.

[1]   Ambrose, Steven. Nothing Like It in the World: *The Men Who Built the Transcontinental Railroad, 1868-1869.* Simon & Schuster, 2001. See index on opium.

[2]   Associated Press. *"No Easy Answers in Traffic Miniseries."*

[3]   *"Beat Generation." Academic American Encyclopedia.* Volume 3. Page 144.

[4]   Browne, Frank. *"Opium." Encyclopedia Britannica,* 1929. Volume 16. Page 811.

[5]   Booth, Martin. *Opium: A History.* St. Martin's Press, 1996. Chapter 4, *"Poverty, Potions and Poppy-heads."* Concerning addicted writers, see especially pages 35-46, 87, 197, 205-206, 213, 219, 215–218, 223-227.

[6]   Brands, H.W. *The Age of Gold: The Gold Rush and the New American Dream.* Anchor, 2003.

[7]   Brecher, Edward. *Licit and Illicit Drugs.* 1989.

[8]   Chan, Anthony. *Perpetually Cool: The Many Lives of Anna May Wong.*

[9]   De Quincey, Thomas. *Confessions of an English Opium Eater.* [1821] Dover, 1996.

[10]   Deep Sea Detectives. *"Gold Rush Disaster: The Frolic."* The History Channel.

[11]   Gleason, Ralph J. *"Lenny Bruce – Live at the Curran Theater: November 19, 1961."* Liner notes to the recording.

[12]   Griffith, William. *Opium Poppy Garden: The Way of a Chinese Grower.* Ronin, 1993. Pages 17-48.

[13]   Gutin, Steven. *"With whips and beard inspections, squads enforce 'pure' Islam in Afghanistan."* Associated Press. June 14, 2001.

[14]   Hart, Hugh. *"Drugs, Bodies, Weapons, and Terrorists." The New York Times Television.* January 21, 2004.

[15]   Hogshire, Jim. *Opium for the Masses.* Loompanics Unlimited, 1994.

[16]   Imhof, John E. [Donald Wigal, editor]. *Drug Education for Teachers and Parents.* Sadlier, 1970.

[17]   *"Jack Kerouac." Academic American Encyclopedia.* Volume 12. Page 59.

[18]   Jacobs, Andrew. *"The Beast in the Bathroom." The New York Times.* January 12, 2004. Page B1.

[19]   Jafee, Jerome. *"Narcotic Analgesics."* In the anthology, *Pharmacological Basis of Therapeutics*. Editors Louis Goodman and Alfred Gilman. Third edition. Macmillan, 1969. Chapter 15.

[20]   Kapoor, L. D. *Opium Poppy: Botany, Chemistry, and Pharmacology.* Food Products Press, 1995. Pages 1-17, 65-94, 255-298.

[21]   Kashner, Sam. *When I was Cool: My Life at the Jack Kerouac School.* Harper Collins, 2004.

[22]   Kolb, Lawrence. *"Drug Addiction."* Encyclopedia Britannica. [1928], Volume 7. Page 676.

[23]   Leonard, Thomas. *Day by Day: The Forties.* Facts on File, 1977.

[24]   Logan, Nick and Bob Woffinden. *The Ilustrated Encyclopedia of Rock.* Harmony, 1977. Pages 72-73.

[25]   Loof, Susan. *"U.N. Agency Warns Afghanistan Over Opium."* The Guardian. October 29, 2003.

[26]   Marquand, Robert. "In China, pews are packed." *Christian Science Monitor.* December 24, 2003.

[27]   Marx, Karl. Introduction to *Contribution to the Critique of Hegel's Philosophy of Right* [1884].

[28]   Maslin, Janet. *"The Twilight of the Beats through an Acolyte's Eyes,"* *The New York Times.* February 5, 2004. A review of Kashner, q.v.

[29]   Meier, Barry. *Pain Killer: A 'Wonder' Drug's Tail of Addiction and Death.* Rodale, 2004. The work is mainly about OxyContin, but it includes background on drugs in general.

[30]   Metzger, T. *The Birth of Heroin and the Demonization of the Dope Fiend.* Loompanics Unlimited, 1998.

[31]   Moore, Wes. *"Hasan Bin Sabbah and the Secret Order of Hashishins."* *Disinformation.* July 6, 2003.

[32]   Muller, Bermann. *Science,* 1955. Page 120.

[33]   NPR. *"Instability Threatens Afghanistan's Future."* National Public Radio; Morning Edition. January 29, 2004.

[34]   Neligan, A. R. *The Opium Question.* Bale and Curnew, 1927. As in Kaapor, op. cit.

[35]   New York City Department of Health and Mental Hygiene. Published Charts.

[36]   *New York Times, "Facing Up to the Inevitable, in Search of a Good Death."* December 30, 2003.

[37]   *Nursing Drug Handbook*. Springhouse, 1986. Page 396.

[38]   O'Hare, Kate. "*'Traffic: The Miniseries Follows the Money.*"

[39]   "*Opium*" and "*Morphine*." *Academic American Encyclopedia*. Arete, 1980.
         Volume13. Opium: Page 587; Volume 14. Morphine: Page 406.

[40]   Preminger, Otto. *Preminger: An Autobiography*. Doubleday, 1977. Page 148.

[41]   Reich, David. "*Managed Death*." *Boston College Magazine*. Spring, 2003. Page 13.

[42]   Scott, J.M. *The White Poppy: A History of Opium*. Funk & Wagnalls, 1969.

[43]   Stuparyk, Melanie. "*Coffee: Heaven-sent or the Devil's Drink.*" *Imprint*. March 13,
         2002. Pages 24: 31.

[44]   Tosches, Nick. *The Last Opium Den*. Bloomsbury, 2002. First published in *Vanity Fair*,
         September, 2000.

[45]   "*Traffic: The Miniseries.*" USA Television Network.

[46]   Turnbull, James J. *Chinese Opium Narcotics*. 1972.

[47]   Veselovskaya, M. A., *The Poppy*. Amerind. From the Russian, 1976.

[48]   VIR. "Death penalty for five heroin and opium smugglers," November 15-21, 1999.

[49]   Walker, Winfred. *The Plants of the Bible*. London, 1959. Page 88. As in Kapoor,
         op. cit.

[50]   Wallace, Irving. "*Small Incidents That Started Big Wars,*" *The People's Almanac*.
         Doubleday, 1975. Page 645.

[51]   Walton, Stuart. "*Random knowledge about drugs.*" *Esquire*, February, 2004. Page 30.
         Quoting Stuart: *Out of It: Cultural History of Intoxication*. Three Rivers Press, 2004.

[52]   Wells, Patrick with Douglas Rushkoff. *Stoned Free: How to Get High Without Drugs*.
         Loompanics Unlimited, 1995.

[53]   Wigal, Donald. *The Visions of Nostradamus and Other Prophets*. Random House,
         1998. Re: Edgar Allen Poe, Pages 90-91; Re: Crowley, Pages 46-47.

[54]   Wigal, Donald. *Historical Maritime Maps Used for Exploration, 1290-1699*,
         Parkstone, 2000. Page 20-21. Also: *Historische Seekarten Entdeckungsfahrten zu
         Neuen Welten*. Parkstone. 2000; *Anciennes Cartes Marines: la Decouverte des
         Nouvaux Mondes*. Parkstone. 2000.

[55]   Wigal, Donald. "*Index,*" *The New York Times Encyclopedia of Film*. Volume 13.

[56]   Willcox, William Henry. "*Drug Addiction*." *Encyclopedia Britannica*. 1928. Volume 7.
         Page 676.